IMAGES
of England

WILLENHALL
TO
HORSELEY FIELDS

The Market Place in Willenhall at the turn of the century, dominated by the Memorial Clock. The market is still held here today, and most of the Victorian buildings remain; only a new block of shops at the far end has imposed on the scene.

A view of Horseley Fields taken from the top of St Peter's church in 1975, before the ring road cut through the area. The Willenhall Road runs to the horizon on the left, and the old Wolverhampton Corporation power station is to the right.

IMAGES
of England

WILLENHALL
TO
HORSELEY FIELDS

Compiled by
Alec Brew

TEMPUS

Willenhall to Horseley Fields is Alec Brew's third book in
The *Archive Photograph* series, chronicling Wolverhampton
in a century of photographs

Also compiled by Alec Brew in The *Archive Photograph* series are:
Codsall and Claregate
Tettenhall and Pattingham
Albrighton and Shifnal
Staffordshire and Black Country Airfields
Penn and Blakenhall
Ettingstall and Monmore Green
Heath Town and Fallings Park
Bushbury and Featherstone
Wolverhampton Pubs

First published 1998
Reprinted 2004

Tempus Publishing Limited
The Mill, Brimscombe Port,
Stroud, Gloucestershire, GL5 2QG
www.tempus-publishing.com

British Library Cataloguing in Publication Data.
A catalogue record for this book is available from the British Library.

ISBN 0 7524 1510 7

Typesetting and origination by Tempus Publishing Limited.
Printed in Great Britain.

Contents

St Giles' church in Walsall Street, Willenhall, as seen in 1904. It was consecrated in 1867, and was the last of a number of churches built on the site.

A Ford Model AF outside Reginald Tildesley's Willenhall depot, on New Road, after a National Reliability Demonstration in April 1929. A bus to Wolverhampton is waiting in the background. The site is now occupied by the Somerfield supermarket.

Introduction

Of all the towns of the Black Country, Willenhall seems to be the one which has changed least over the years. Walking around the town, it is still possible to see most of the buildings which feature in the oldest photographs in this book. Neither the developers nor the Luftwaffe demolished large areas, as they did in so many other Black Country towns; though perhaps new changes will follow the contraction of Willenhall's most important industry.

Most Black Country towns are famous for one particular industry, and Willenhall is perhaps the best example of this, being world-famous for the production of locks. It is home to all the most famous names in the industry, Legge, Josiah Parkes, Squire, Yale and John Harper's. The trade started as a back-yard industry, with one man or one family workshops, and many of these small companies survived until recently, despite the competition of the big names. One such operation is preserved in Willenhall's marvellous Lock Museum.

With much of its population bending over vices all day, Willenhall earned itself the nickname, 'Humpshire', derived from the humps its workforce are supposed to have developed. A catalogue of jokes at Willenhall inhabitant's expense resulted, such as the fact that Willenhall pubs have holes in their walls for their customer's humps.

Though the town is now part of the Borough of Walsall, it is nearer to Wolverhampton and most residents of Humpshire look here for big town shopping and services. At the other end of the Willenhall to Wolverhampton road, which was the lock industry axis, lies one of the biggest players in the industry, Chubb.

The last part of this road runs through the Wolverhampton suburb of Horseley Fields, once a thriving community with its own shops, cinema and major companies, such as the Chillington Tool Company, British Oxygen, and the Ever Ready factory. The Ever Ready factory had previously been occupied by AJS, and before that Briton Cars.

Crowded around these factories were terraced houses, in some cases the most deprived in the town, and the churches, chapels, shops and other businesses that served them. This community has almost totally disappeared now, and this is highlighted by the shrunken size of what was once Willenhall Road school. When my mother went there it was divided into three parts, infants, juniors and seniors, with over 1,000 pupils. Now it is just a junior school with a couple of hundred students, and the other large local school, in Walsall Street, has totally disappeared.

There has long been controversy as to whether the area should in fact be Horseley Fields or Horseley Field, and this was discussed in particular in the war years. There were letters to the local paper arguing each case, but the answer is rather simple. There are two areas to the suburb, Horseley Field and Lower Horseley Field, harking back to agricultural days, and together they make up Horseley Fields, in the plural.

Nowadays, the communities of Willenhall and Horseley Fields are merged together in one large conurbation, infilled by the new estates of East Park, Moseley and Deansfield. I was born just after the Second World War, at my grandmother's house at 54, Coventry Street, just off the Willenhall Road, and beyond the end of the garden there was nothing but fields and trees stretching as far as the Portobello area of Willenhall. That there was a thriving farming community surrounding Willenhall, is highlighted by the fact that Reginald Tildesley had a large Fordson tractor dealership in the town, though they also sold Ford cars and vans. The company still operates, but no longer finds much of a market for tractors in the area.

The farms have gone, replaced by new housing and industrial estates. Even some of these have become 'brownfield sites' as the traditional industries struggle to survive. Lock making seems to have fared better than many other industries in the Black Country, but now even that is feeling the pinch. Nevertheless, it is not every town which is famous throughout the world for its products and the particular skills of its people. This alone should make the residents of Humpshire proud of the town of Willenhall.

Alec Brew
April 1998

One

Willenhall
Before 1945

In the Middle Ages the countryside south of Wolverhampton was an underpopulated, forested area, but then iron and coal were discovered and the forests made way for the fiery holes of the Black Country. The lock-making trade took hold in Bilston, Wolverhampton and in particular the small town of Willenhall. Locks were made by hand in small workshops dotted about the town, until the invention of production machinery in the late Victorian times. Large companies with World-famous names began to take hold of the business and the little town of Willenhall supplied locks for the Empire and the rest of the World.

The busy centre of Willenhall, at the turn of the century, with a single-decker tram arriving from Wolverhampton along New Road. New Road was built around 1818, to improve communications with Wolverhampton.

The old St Giles church which was demolished to make way for the present building in 1865. Willenhall was originally part of the parish of Wolverhampton and all burials had to take place there before 1727. Willenhall did not become a parish in its own right until 1840. The three-storey vicarage alongside the church was demolished early in this century after falling into disrepair.

Stafford Street, before the First World War, looking south towards the Market Place. The Plough Inn has the double bow windows on the left. It is said that prisoners sentenced by Willenhall magistrates were allowed to stop here for one last drink on their way to Stafford Gaol.

A motorcycle rally with the participants lined up across New Road, in 1911. From left to right: Reg Tonks, Bernard Roberts, Aloisius Jones, William Bishop, Latimer Wedge, Harry Wedge, Moses Jobborn, Harold Tipper, Arthur Davies.

A railway accident at Neachell's Junction, Willenhall, on the Midland Railway, which took place on 17 October 1899. The photograph shows smashed passenger coaches and the engine on its side.

The passenger train collided with a goods train, and this photograph shows the de-railed trucks on the embankment.

The inauguration of the Memorial Clock in the Market Place on 10 May 1892. It was built in the memory of Dr Joseph Tonks, a much-respected local doctor. From left to right: C.H. Pinson, John Roddis, Isaac Pedley, William Johnson, George Baker, James Carpenter Tildesley, and George Parkes.

The Brown Jug Inn at Sandbeds, Willenhall, around 1910. The publican and his wife, Mr and Mrs Rowland Richards, stand in the doorway. Many of their customers will have worked in the brick, tile and pipe works set up in 1899, to exploit the rich clay on Sand-Beds Farm.

Two travellers outside the George & Crown Inn, on Bilston Road, in 1913. Isaac Bissell was the publican at the time.

The celebrations for the Coronation of King George V in 1911. A crowd of people are precariously balanced on a makeshift balcony over the door of the Central Café in the Market Place.

The New Church schools next to St Giles', on the Walsall Road, just after their opening in 1908. The building is now known as St Giles' C.E. primary school.

The Council Schools at Portobello, before the First World War. They were built next to the bridge over the L&NW railway line. The imposing bell tower has now been demolished and the building is in use as a community centre.

Group 3 from the Russell Street Primitive Methodist school, in the year 1902.

The Central Schools were for 11 to 14-year-old pupils and this is Standard VI in 1912. The class was separated with the boys to the left and girls to the right; the teacher, Mr Rogers, is in the background.

The Willenhall Swifts football team in the year they were formed, at the rear of the Bird in the Hand pub, in 1899.

The Swifts in the 1905-6 season. They are seen in their new blue and white stripes, which graced the ground in Temple Road. They were a semi-professional club, and rivals to the older Willenhall club, the Pickwicks.

Children in the Primitive Methodist's church in Russell Street, celebrating 'Junior Endeavour Worldwide', around the year 1904.

The Shakespeare Inn, Somerford, the original home of the Willenhall Pickwicks football club. The publican, Job Broadbent is sitting with his dog 'Turk'.

The Willenhall fire brigade outside their headquarters in Clemson Street, just before the First World War. Ike Smith, the man on the back row, to the far right, kept the alarm bell by his bed in Gomer Street, and his wife used to wrap the clapper up to reduce the shock when it rang.

The rear of the Old Hall which was the birthplace of Dr Richard Wilkes (1690-1760). He practised as a doctor without any training though, and also became a local historian. His father had built the Hall, which the Wilkes family sold in 1789. It was demolished in 1934 to make way for Willenhall Town Hall.

THE MANOR, WILLENHALL. NO. 802.

The Manor, before the First World War. This was a residential development which drew its name from the Leveson Family's Moat House. It was the largest house in Willenhall, on Moat Street, and was often called the Manor House.

THE MANOR, WILLENHALL.

Another view of part of the Manor Estate, showing how quiet life used to be, when the only traffic in either picture is a wheelbarrow!

A single-decker Wolverhampton Corporation tram outside the Cleveland Road depot, about to travel the route through Horseley Fields to Willenhall.

Tram tracks, running along the cobbles of New Road with the tower of the Council Schools, Portobello in the distance. This was originally a turnpike, and the toll house still exists, between the TSB and National Westminster banks.

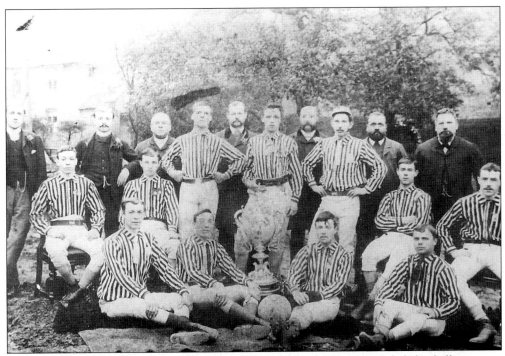

Willenhall Pickwicks football club. 'The Picks', were the first recorded football team in Willenhall, having been formed in the mid 1880s. They played in Portobello with red and white striped shirts, but the date of this photograph is not known.

'The Picks' deadly rivals were the Willenhall Swifts, shown here in 1907, after winning the Walsall League Cup, the Wednesbury Charity Cup and the Staffordshire League Cup. It is clear that the goalkeeper was picked for his height, and the player on his right looks like the hard-man of the team.

Children of St Ann's school, *c.* 1926. The school and church were in Ann Street, off St Ann's Road, Springbank. In the front row, from the left: Phoebe Babb, Joseph Lockley, Alice Blewitt, Victor Morgan, the rest are unknown. In the middle row, third from the right, is Marjorie Wade.

A section of Neachell's Lane, known as The Twenty Trees, taken around 1910. The cart possibly belonged to Neachell's Farm which was near to the railway. It is a purely industrial area these days; how quickly such rural tranquillity disappeared.

St Giles church, viewed from The Wakes Ground, *c.* 1910. The Willenhall Wakes Week traditionally featured Pat Collins' Fair on the Wakes Ground.

A rare side view of Bentley Hall, the home of the Lane family, taken in 1907. In 1651 King Charles II, fled from the Battle of Worcester. Having already hidden at Boscobel House, he was met by Colonel John Lane at Moseley Hall, Wolverhampton, and escorted to Bentley Hall.

The old St Stephen's church, which was built on Wolverhampton Street, six years after the parish was created out of Wolverhampton parish, in 1854. This church was demolished in 1978, and replaced by a new building. The original site is now occupied by St Stephen's Court flats.

The Metropolitan Bank on the corner of New Road and Market Place, c. 1910. It is now the Midland Bank.

A section of Walsall Street before widening operations were undertaken in the 1920s.

During the First World War, Ike Smith of
Gomer Street exchanged his fireman's uniform
for that of the Staffordshire Regiment.

: : NATIONAL : :
SIEGE OF SOULS

THE SALVATION ARMY, Willenhall

SUNDAY, November 21, 1915,

Commissioner EDWARD J.
HIGGINS

(Territorial Leader, Salvation Army Forces, United Kingdom)

will conduct Meetings as follows:

.. IN ..

THE PICTURE HOUSE,
STAFFORD STREET,

11 a.m. and 6.45 p.m., SALVATION.

3 p.m., Topic :

'The Salvation Army in Peace and War'

Chairman : ENOCH TONKS, Esq., J.P.
(Chairman of the Council),
supported by a number of influential Ladies and Gentlemen.

You are invited ! ∴ **Song Sheets provided !**

The Commissioner has been an Officer of The Salvation Army for over 30 years, has travelled all over the world and occupied most important positions in various Countries, and at present is the Territorial Commissioner of The Army in the United Kingdom. He possesses rich stores of information and is a most acceptable public speaker.

The Salvation Army Printing Works, St. Albans

The British Army was not the only organization recruiting during the First World War, as shown by this poster for the Salvation Army.

Commissioner Edward J. Higgins of the Salvation Army was, according to the accompanying poster, the possessor of rich stores of information and a most acceptable public speaker. The Sally Army had first assaulted Willenhall in 1881, with great success, and a 'wooden cathedral' had been built in Moat Street.

Bentley Hall, between Willenhall and Walsall. It was not only King Charles II who sought refuge here, but John Wesley was 'carried there by the Wednesbury mob'. It has long since been demolished to make way for a housing estate.

Two huge boards in front of 33 Market Place, next to the Bell Inn, in July 1918. They show that £204,309 had been raised so far, to buy 81 aircraft, which means that they cost just over £2,500 each. This will have been the full cost including engine, whereas in the Second World War a town only had to raise a nominal £5,000 to 'buy' a Spitfire.

To celebrate the 'final score' of £204,309 raised, a military band is seen playing in the Market Place, where a vast crowd has gathered to hear the announcement. Henly & Co., the ironmongers, seen in the background are still trading today.

The Willenhall War Memorial erected at the corner of Stafford Street and Field Street to commemorate the 443 Willenhall men who lost their lives in the First World War.

The official opening of the new Willenhall Town Hall, on the site of Old Hall, on 20 March 1935. Willenhall Urban District Council had been formed in 1894, and was to remain independent until swallowed up by Walsall Borough.

Willenhall Town Hall as it originally looked. The railings have gone, and the building is now the public library.

Members of Willenhall Urban District Council seated outside the door of the Town Hall, around 1948.

Portobello railway bridge, before widening, in the 1920s. The tram is on its way to Wolverhampton, and a traffic island now occupies the site of the houses beyond the bridge.

Children of Little London school, during the 1920s.

Children at Central school, around 1919. The only known name is Harry Shepherd, on the second row back, fifth from the right.

Children in the playground of Little London school, possibly on Empire Day. The figure of 'Britannia' in the centre is Joyce Spate, aged 10 years.

Reginald Tildesley staff, with a Ford Model AF that had covered 1,800 miles non-stop, in a three-day reliability trial. The board proudly boasts of a petrol consumption of 30.5 mpg, which was very reasonable, and an oil consumption of 1,200 mpg, which is unbelievable. From left to right: Harold Pyatt, George Harley, Reg Williams, Harry Bond, Bert Wyke (who was Reg Tildesley's first employee in 1919), Fred Chenners.

Reginald Tildesley's car workshops in Willenhall. The huge Lincoln on the right was Tildesley's own car, and the one in which he was killed. Tildesley opened his garage on New Road before the First World War, initially selling different makes, but in 1912 it became a Ford dealership.

A Ford AA truck ready for delivery to Stubbs, Barratt & Co. of Bilston Street, Wolverhampton on 31 August 1929.

Darlaston District Council's new ambulance awaiting delivery at Tildesley's. Speeding over cobbled streets in this must have been uncomfortable for someone with broken bones!

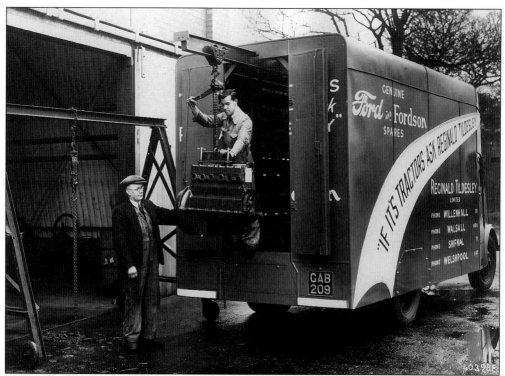

Tildesley's mobile workshop was a very useful piece of equipment for repairing tractors all over Shropshire and Staffordshire. As can be seen on the side, the company also had depots in Shifnal, Walsall and Welshpool.

The Picture House in Stafford Street, when seats were 2d, 3d and 6d, during the First World War. One of the posters exhorts 'It's our Flag, Fight for it, Work for it!'

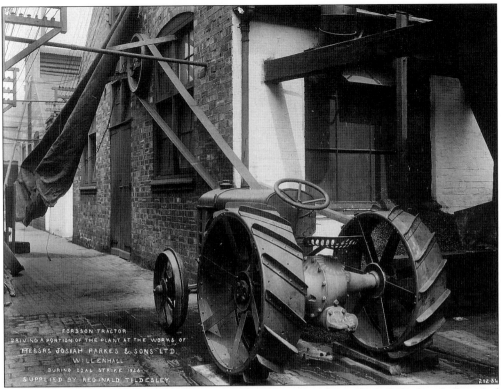

A Fordson Model F tractor, being used to drive part of the plant of Josiah Parkes & Sons Ltd during the coal strike of 1926.

Tildesley's tractor workshops, around 1937. The engines are reconditioned units. Tildesley sold his first Fordson tractor in 1922.

The Willenhall lodge of the Ancient Order of Sherwood Foresters. The Chief Ranger was Ike Smith, seated third from the left.

Union Locks football team, in the early 1930s.

A charabanc outing from Willenhall to Matlock, in the 1920s. They might have been employees of the Walsall Lock Co. as Thomas Spate, who is seated next to the second window, worked for them, but he was also a member of the Order of Sherwood Foresters. Thomas Spate, who lived in St Stephen's Avenue died in 1934, from ulcers caused by mustard gas in the trenches.

Another charabanc belonging to J.H. Wedge & Co, of Stafford Street, Willenhall.

The centre of Willenhall on a rainy day. The policeman seems to be looking around for traffic to direct. The building behind has by now become the Midland Bank.

Stafford Street railway sidings, with a large shipment of Fordson tractors for Tildesley's. The tractors were shipped to Stafford Street because there were better off-loading facilities than at Bilston Road, which was right behind Tildesley's Depot.

The Ambulance (First Aid) class of the London, Midland, Scottish Railway, Willenhall, in 1926-7.

The Cemetery Road North railway bridge, before widening, with a J. Brevitt & Co. truck crossing, in the 1920s. Josiah Brevitt had started as a carrier during the last century, delivering parcels for his father Joseph, who was a key maker. This was then extended to deliveries for others.

The Willenhall town band between the wars, with Bandmaster W.E. Webster seated in the centre.

Hauling coal by horse and cart. The man seated holding the reins owned the business.

A lifeboat being hauled around Willenhall as part of the National Lifeboat appeal in 1930. It had been fetched from Birmingham by Fred Chennels of Tildesley's who is standing behind the tractor with Mr Ward.

Willenhall Town football club, between the wars. Former players and officials of the Swifts and the Pickwicks formed the club after the First World War.

Reginald Tildesley's display at the 1926 West Midlands Agricultural Show. The Ford Coupe, first in the row under the awning, was going for the princely sum of £170. The Fordson Quintet gang mower was priced at £82.50.

A GWR charabanc on a trip from Willenhall to Brecon, where this photograph was taken. The conductor was Mr Greenhill of Willenhall.

A Group of Willenhall Urban District Council employees photographed between the wars.

These Trains are subject to Co's. alterations.

L. & N. W. Ry.		Wolverhampton. Willenhall, and Walsall.																	
W'hampton	556	720	822	928	1040	1110	1241	131	246	—	345	455	515	528	734	9 4	936	1050	1128
Willenhall	6 3	726	829	936	1047	1117	1249	137	253	—	352	5 1	523	535	742	915	942	1056	1134
Walsall	615	738	841	951	1059	1129	1 2	150	3 7	—	4 4	513	537	547	755	929	955	11.9	1147
Walsall ...	713	825	913	9 43	1037	1055	1141	1213	121	146	346	428	527	610	636	753	820	—	9 58	1036
Willenhall	722	835	923	9 52	1046	11 5	1151	1222	131	156	356	437	537	621	645	8 5	830	854	10 8	1046
W'hampton	731	843	933	10 1	1055	1116	12 1	1233	142	2 5	4 6	449	547	630	659	814	840	9 5	1020	1058

To Birmingham.							† 1210 Saturdays.					From Birmingham.						
W'hampton	732	810	852	1018	1227	110	—	435	558	621		Birmingham	733	815	932	†1215	115	420	650	725	840
Willenhall	739	817	859	1026	1230	117	240	441	6 6	628		Bescot {arr	8 0	846	959	1244	143	446	7 7	756	9 7
Bescot {arr	750	828	911	1037	1245	128	250	451	617	639		{dep	835	852	10 0	1252	154	455	712	8 2	914
{dep	8 0	839	926	1048	1256	139	3 4	452	633	641		Willenhall	846	9 3	1012	1 1	2 5	5 5	724	813	924
Birmingham	830	911	955	1116	1 25	211	332	528	7 3	—		W'hampton	857	915	1025	110	—	514	734	—	938

MIDLAND TRAINS.

					Sundays										Sundays			
W'hampton	950	1215	629	8 0		938	1055	9 4		Birmingham	724	112	—	—		—	9 25	730
Willenhall	10 2	1227	642	812		946	11 4	912		Walsall	850	215	—	617		842	1017	819
Walsall	1017	1250	659	825		959	1121	932		Willenhall	850	229	—	631		854	1030	832
Birmingham	—	2 7	—	—		—	12 6	1014		W'hampton	9 1	238	—	640		9 2	1037	839

The 1926 railway timetable shows that Willenhall citizens had a choice of railways on which to travel to Birmingham or Wolverhampton. One of the businesses advertised: the funeral directors, Thomas Ely & Co., still operates today.

Class III at Willenhall Central school, in 1920. The lad marked with a cross is Harry Shepherd.

Willenhall post office in Wolverhampton Street, just off the Market Place.

Lock making is the industry for which Willenhall is world-famous and this is part of the factory of one of the great names in the industry, Josiah Parkes, in 1922.

Another part of the Josiah Parkes' factory in 1922. The photograph shows that women were also employed in some numbers. Note the machinery driven by belts from overhead shafts.

H.S. Nicklin's greengrocers shop at 11 Stafford Street, in 1923.

Shaw Foundry Company's employees and their children with the company float for the Willenhall Carnival. Shaw's was a general brass and iron foundry making locks, builder's hardware and brassware in their Denver works.

R.W. Longstaffe's drapery shop in Cross Street.

E. Fortnam's corn merchants in Wolverhampton Street, in the 1920s.

The work force of Messrs Charles Perry, at The Croft, in the 1920s.

The float of Arthur Shaw & Co., Denver Works, Willenhall. 'The Denver Follies' were taking part in the Wolverhampton Carnival and were photographed by West Park, c. 1936.

Willenhall's Memorial Park was built on derelict land and opened in 1922. That is clearly the year this picture was taken. The open countryside on the far side of the park at the time is very obvious in this picture.

A view of the Memorial Park looking in the other direction, showing the bandstand, which became a big attraction.

Joyce Spate, on the right, and Marjorie Clifford at the Carnival in the Memorial Park. In the background is Tom Spate's Balloon Race stall.

Tom Spate's balloon race stall, on a lorry entitled 'Con a Copper Bost a Blether', a translation from the 'Humpshire' is not available. Joyce Spate is on the lorry holding the balloons and her uncle, Albert Hodson, is standing next to her.

Willenhall poor children's outing in the 1920s.

One of the Willenhall Carnival floats in 1925. The Carnival was a major town event between the wars and lots of organizations would have floats in the parade which wound around town. It ended in the Memorial Park where the judging of the floats took place.

The well-known Round House on Walsall Road, sited where the turnpike gate used to be. By 1929 it was a restaurant, as it is today, and renamed Ye Olde Toll House. Next door is Frank Lloyd & Sons, motor body builder, which had evolved from being a blacksmiths of long standing.

'The Comic Band', parading in the Carnival of 1929.

Mr C.V. Sheyvn, standing at the door of his grocery shop in the 1930s. The shop was next to
The Cock Inn, on the north side of Portobello High Street.

Mr Fontana at the door of his cigarettes and sweet shop in Stafford Street. Mr Fontana was an Italian who sold very good ice cream.

The Methodist church in Union Street, which was completed in this form in 1863. There had been a chapel on the site from 1810. The building is now the Trinity Methodist church, dating from when the various branches of the Methodists united in 1966.

A page of advertisements from the town guide. More than half the businesses advertising in the guide were connected with the lock industry.

The opening of the new Drill Hall for D Company of the South Staffordshire Regiment, on 22 March 1924. Colonel J.V. Campbell of the Coldstream Guards is inspecting the troops.

Clarkes Lane after road widening took place in the 1920s. The entrance to John Harper's lock factory is on the left.

A view of the Memorial Park in the 1930s. By now the trees and bushes have begun to grow into a beautiful park. The town has recently won a National Lottery grant to restore the park to its former glory.

The Dale cinema on the other side of the New Road from the Market Place, which was showing *The Desert Song* at the time. It was built on the site of the Coliseum, the first cinema in Willenhall, but which lost out in competition with The Picture House in Stafford Street. It is now the Dale bingo hall.

St Mary's Roman Catholic school camp at Paradise Camp in Coven, just north of Wolverhampton in 1936. Paradise Camp was used by a number of Willenhall organizations to give summer holidays to local children.

Another group of Willenhall girls at Paradise Camp. Mrs Francis Spate is sitting on the steps, with Miss Dorothy Butler standing behind her. Peeping round the door is Gladys Parker.

The Willenhall Wesleyan Girls Life Brigade at camp in 1933; whether it is also at Coven is unknown. Joyce Spate is on the left of the back row.

The combined choir of St Giles' and St Matthew's churches marching on to the Willenhall Wakes ground for a Sunday concert, c. 1935. There are fairground stalls all around.

Gomer Street, Willenhall, decorated either for the Jubilee or the Coronation in the 1930s.

Workers at Baker's Lock Co. which was situated on Moat Street, Willenhall. The photograph was taken in 1939.

The Lane Head Methodist chapel bowling 'B' team, who were the winners of the Willenhall and District Church and Chapel League, in 1939. In the back row, from left to right: R. Marsh, R. Whitehouse, and H. Wood. In the second row: V. Squire, A. Lockley, J. Birch, A. Birch, W. Evans, A. Ratcliffe, and H. Clift. In the front row: F. Birch, E. Squire, J. Humphries, H. Worrall, and P. Birch.

Willenhall Cubs camp at Brewood in 1939. The lad on the back row, on the extreme right is John Wright.

A parade from St Giles' church for Girl Guide Week, in May 1939.

Willenhall air raid victims being buried in November 1940. A sadder parade than that of the Girl Guides seen only a few months before.

The Willenhall Spitfire, bought with £6,760 raised by the town. It was not a Hurricane, as noted in this commemorative postcard, but a Spitfire Mk.VB, serial AB251.

The site of a Spitfire crash-landing in Willenhall on 18 April 1942. Alex Henshaw, the chief test pilot at the Shadow Factory at Castle Bromwich, was flying Spitfire EP615 back from RAF Cosford. At 800 ft over Willenhall, his engine stopped dead. He spotted a piece of greenery and attempted a wheels-up landing, but the starboard wing stalled and hit the tree on the right.

The starboard wing snapped off and the Spitfire swung into the house in the background; the engine crashing through the kitchen wall. The house is believed to be near to Stubby Lane.

The two ladies are looking towards the remains of the aircraft which came to rest beyond the house. Once Henshaw realized he was not badly hurt he scrambled rapidly from the shattered wreckage. The lady of the house tremulously asked how many more were in the aircraft and was re-assured that it was a single seater. An old man with shaking hands, brought over a cup of tea laced with whisky, but when Henshaw said he did not drink, the man gulped it down himself!

The Willenhall Home Guard posing on the dog track in 1943. Willenhall was originally part of the huge South Staffordshire Battalion. The dog track doubled as the football ground and was situated just behind Portobello school.

The Willenhall ATC Band marching with the Home Guard through Upper Green, Tettenhall, with Colonel Parkes taking the salute.

The Golden Wedding Anniversary of Florence and Bill Fisher in 1943. They had seven sons, standing left to right: Jim, Harry, Joe, Frank, Fred (who was be killed in Holland in January 1945), Jack and Bill. They also had three daughters, seated, left to right: Clara, Betty and Louie. The Fishers kept a pub in Willenhall. Mrs Fisher, who had been born Marsh, had a twin sister, Clara, who married Bernard Moseley of Short Heath. Clara also had ten children, seven boys and three girls!

C Company of the Willenhall Home Guard, photographed around 1943.

Two
Willenhall
After 1945

A few years ago, when I worked in Nigeria for a construction company, one of my duties was to do the local buying. When I needed to buy some locks I naturally looked for familiar British brands such as Union Locks. In the market I would pick up a box which was ostensibly a Union product, but on close examination would see that the lettering actually read 'Unine' Lock, or 'Onion' lock, it had the same design of box, the same colours, but had definitely not originated from Willenhall. Even those which said 'Union' on them were very often not the real thing, nor were they 'Legge' locks, the other main brand to be found. This was both a tribute to Willenhall, acknowledging the town's products as being the finest in the world, and also part of its downfall, with cheap Far East imitations flooding the markets of the Third World. The local locksmith had been trained in Willenhall, and was happy to discover I had been born 'next-door'. Whenever there was a burglary in the town, when there was no sign of breaking and entry, the police came and arrested him. Even though they always let him go, he was getting pretty sick of it. The skills acquired in Humpshire were both his living and his curse.

Employees of Josiah Parkes and Co., just after the war, the occasion and location are unknown.

Willenhall Carnival parade goes past the Co-op, more recently Blockbuster video. The Yale float is mounted on a gun carriage.

The Fifth Willenhall Boy Scouts Band in 1946. They had inherited the drums of the Willenhall Home Guard, hence the crest of the South Staffordshire Regiment 2/6th Battalion. Third from the left is John Wright, on his left is Reg Greenhill, then Chris Richards and Alan Clarke.

The Fifth Willenhall Boy Scouts in Derbyshire, in 1945. The tallest one, on the extreme left, is John Wright.

A group of Willenhall Council workers on an outing to Blackpool during the 1950s. Albert Kershaw, fifth from the right, worked for the Council for twenty-five years, before his death in 1964.

B.E. Wedge Ltd, the galvanizers of Stafford Street, operated this Morris Commercial.

Union Locks cricket team, during the 1950s.

Some of the ladies on Fox & Morgan's outing to Blackpool, in 1946 or 1947.

Two diesel rail units leaving Willenhall's Bilston Street station. Doctor Beeching ended passenger services to Willenhall, but the recent re-opening of the Wolverhampton to Walsall line brings hope of their return.

Brickkiln Street in Portobello during 1972. This was just before the street was demolished, to make way for the dual carriageway road to Wolverhampton.

The High Street, Portobello, looking East towards Willenhall in 1972. This was also just about to be demolished to make way for the dual carriageway. The pub is The Gough Arms.

The High Street Portobello looking west towards Wolverhampton. Note the trolley bus wires overhead, these had replaced the trams back in 1931. Portobello became part of the Borough of Wolverhampton in 1966 while the rest of Willenhall joined Walsall Borough.

The bottom end of the Market Place, Willenhall in the 1960s. It looks much as it did fifty years before, apart from the intrusion of cars but even these have gone again now after pedestrianization.

The top end of the Market Place where it narrows to become Stafford Street and the new block of shops which is the one piece of redevelopment which intrudes on what is now a listed square.

Reginald Tildesley's Willenhall depot decorated for the Coronation in 1953. The Dale cinema is visible behind.

The St Giles' Youth Club second XI football team in 1966/7. Standing, from left to right: Ray Burns, Mick Tafano, Peter Morris, Charlie Watson, Tony Bryan, -?-, and Alan Barnard. Kneeling: Trevor Eaton, Suka Singh, John Wedge, Paul Bryan and Stanley Mann.

John Harper's Albion Works football team of 1951. Arthur Garbett is on the front row, second from the left.

The first year of Willenhall Comprehensive, in 1956. The teachers are: Mr Wright who taught physics and Miss Rounds who taught biology. The only known names are on the back row, second from the left: Michael Turner, and on the middle row, from left to right: Barry Tomlinson, Mervyn Pitt, -?-, Janet Dunning, Dorothy Perkins, Christine Moore, Ian Mills, Donald McKay and -?-. On the front row: -?-, -?-, Ann Parsons, Glenise Fisher, -?-, -?-, -?-, Jill Timmins, -?-, Lynn Morgan.

Stan Cullis, the famous Wolves player and manager is seen cutting the tape to open Willenhall town's new Noose Lane ground in April 1975. To his right stand the Wolves player Derek Parkin and Willenhall secretary Tony Turpin.

Form 8 of the Central secondary modern school Willenhall, in October 1949. On the back row, from left to right: Eddowes, Russell, Johnson, Summerfield, Stokes, Harbach, Porton, White, Randle, and Holmes. On the middle row: Swift, Vicarage, Carney, Green, Saunders, Millington, Jordan, Price, Biddulph, Martin, Lockley, and Groucutt. On the front row: Haddon, Cooper, Fox, Burns, Wynn, Reynolds, Alinson, -?-, Groucutt, Cheer, Charnock, Williams, Price, Addison, -?-.

St George's Day Parade, going by St Giles' church, and holding up the trolley bus from Walsall on 5 May 1962.

Willenhall Council employees in 1965-6. On the back row, from left to right: Mr Ridyard (building inspector), Maurice Hughes (committee clerk), John Riding (clerk of the council), Mr Sarnie (legal department), Mr Barnes (deputy clerk), Keith Walker (legal department), Mr Cotterill (architects department), -?- (housing department). On the front row: Joan Howells (Mr Barnes secretary), Pam Kellock (Mr Ridings secretary), Jeanette ? (surveyor's costing clerk), Carol Loder (secretary to clerks), Mabel Turley (surveyors costing clerk), Dorothy ? (secretary to legal department).

St Giles' keep fit class, *c.* 1978. However, what they are doing on the scaffolding is nobody's business.

Willenhall Town football team, with the West Midlands League First Division Championship Shield, 1975/6. On the back row, from left to right: Gordon Edwards, Gary Matthews, Barry Bradshaw, Losh Kelly, Phil Harper, Jess Vorley, and John Newell. On the front row: Gary Stevens, Micky Gunter, Peter Sturgess, Richie Dams, and Peter Willets.

Noose Lane, before there was a football ground, or much else there. The area had been bought by the construction company, Shellabear-Price and in 1938/9 they were levelling and filling in all the old mine workings, which covered the area. The houses dimly seen in the distance are on Neachell's Lane.

An Albion Lorry belonging to Plascom Grout, of 180 Willenhall Road, Wolverhampton.

A Wolverhampton Corporation trolley bus waiting for passengers in Bilston Street. It was bound for Fighting Cocks, Wolverhampton in 1965.

Two

Horseley Fields

Horseley Fields used to be a suburb that I viewed from the top of a trolley bus going from Queen Square to my grandmother's house in Coventry Street. It was a large inner city suburb like many others, a town within a town, full of people and full of life, with everything its inhabitants needed to live, work and play, but now it has all but disappeared.Some of the companies remain, some of the churches, and even a few of the houses, but it has lost its identity. It has no heart any more, no central spine around which the community had thrived. People still pass through it to get to Coventry Street, and beyond that to the new estates and to Willenhall, but when they stare out from the top of the bus, one thing they no longer see is people. I hope this book helps recall the days when Horseley Fields, both of them, were home to thousands of people, to an entire community which has now been largely dispersed.

Horseley Field, looking toward the centre of Wolverhampton with St Peter's in the distance, in the 1960s. All of this has now gone, buildings, trolley buses, and even window cleaners who carry their ladders on a cart.

Near the end of Horseley Field is Wolverhampton station, shown here in its first incarnation in 1907. It is seen as Wolverhampton High Level serving both the LNWR and the Midland Railway.

This is the other end of the 'lock-making axis', Chubb's lock works face High Level station, a few yards from the end of Horseley Field. This was photographed before the First World War. The buildings used to be the workhouse and were a barracks for a time before Chubb's moved in.

For many years one of the largest employers in Wolverhampton was the Chillington Tool Company of Hickman Avenue, making agricultural implements and tools. This is the whole workforce in 1888, with their employer, Mr J.W. Hunt, inset.

In 1912, Edward Lisle Jnr moved the Briton Motor Company from the premises of his father's company, Star Engineering, to Lower Walsall Street. Briton had been formed to produce a cheaper range of cars than Star, like these shown in the Lower Walsall Street factory. The company went into liquidation in 1922 and the factory was sold to AJS.

The centenary of Mount Zion chapel, Horseley Field, in 1910. One of the elders (third from the left) in the front row is Thomas Frost, the Wolverhampton shopfitter.

F. Jennings & Sons were established in Horseley Field in 1848. They are still there today, although they are in new premises. This picture shows a horse-drawn hearse outside 16 St James Street with F. Jennings Snr and Jack Jennings. Behind are F. Jennings Jnr and Thomas Picken, the groom, on the carriage.

The edge tool makers at the Chillington Tool Company, in 1888. The symbol of the company was 'the crocodile' and things like machetes for the Empire were a common product, as well as garden tools like hoes and spades.

The warehouse department at Chillington Tool Co., in 1901. On the back row, from left to right: Tom Hitch, Sarah Booth, George Heath, Ethel Jackson, Joe Green, Eliza Steele, Sidney Monckton, Dave Lavell, and W. Porter (holding Rose the dog). On the front row: Sarah Pritchard, Eliza Pritchard, Lily Chinn, Arthur Parkes, Minnie Jackson, Harriett Rogers and Esther Bodley.

Chillington Tool Co. engineering staff in 1903. On the back row, from left to right: J. Gandy, A. Fisher, J. Delve, J. Halfpenny, W. Thomas, J. Brown, and H. Webb. On the front row: T. Gandy, G. Fisher, J. Hopkins, W. Fisher, and J. Vincent.

The interior of the Bethel chapel alongside the Willenhall Road, when there was a communion rail around the pulpit, around the turn of the century.

The wedding of J. Colbourne, leader of the Bethel chapel. On the back row, from left to right: -?-, J. Brown, A. Crowe, M. Crowe, -?-, J. Colbourne, Mrs. Colbourne, -?-, -?-, -?-, and A. Colbourne. On the front row: Florrie Hopton, Agnes Griffiths, -?-, -?-, Liz Brown, Annie Griffiths, and -?-. The children in the picture are unknown.

The coming of age party of Mr J.K. Hunt, son of the founder of the Chillington Tool Company, held in the old Agricultural Hall, in 1904. The Agricultural Hall, which was demolished in 1907 was on the site later occupied by the Gaumont cinema, at the bottom of Snow Hill.

An outing from the Bethel chapel, in the 1920s. In the picture are (but not necessarily in this order!): -?-, George Elmore, George Lloyd, Mr Caddick, Cyril Cox, Mr Hopley, E. Williams, A. Broome, W. Davies, A. Colbourne, K. Williams, J. Wilkes, J. Hammersley, B. Hopley, J. Hopley, H. Broome, and J. Worthington.

The railway bridge over Lower Horseley Field in 1929. This was taken before the road had been lowered for double-decker buses. The factory on the right was previously Briton Motors and by now was AJS, making cars and radios.

The bandstand in East Park, built on the other side of Hickman Avenue, from the Chillington Tool Company. East Park served the people of Horseley Fields to one side and the Monmore Green area to the other.

Although always regarded as a poorer facility than West Park, on the other side of Wolverhampton, no expense was spared when East Park was built, as can be seen in this 1907 picture. Unfortunately though, the pool always leaked into the old mine workings underground and had dried up by 1906. The clock tower has since been demolished.

A Sunday school outing from the Bethel chapel, in the 1920s. On the back row, from left to right: May Lowbridge, Mrs Solloway, -?-, -?-, -?-, Mrs Florrie Griffiths, and Doris Lapridge. On the front row: Mr Caddick, John Griffiths, Gladys Caddick, -?-, and -?-.

George Bickley in AJS's yard in Lower Walsall Street, *c.* 1923. He is sitting on his Cotton motorcycle though, not an AJS. George was latterly the chauffeur to Charles Hayward, and often drove Mrs Hayward and young Jack, now Sir Jack Hayward.

The local Boys Brigade at the church parade on the Mayor's Sunday at St Peter's in Wolverhampton, *c.* 1929.

Terraced houses in Corser Street, which was just off Lower Horseley Field, and backed on to St Matthew's church, taken in 1929.

An aerial view of the Chillington Tool Co., photographed in 1928. Hickman Avenue runs across the top of the picture.

Workers pouring in to work at Chillington Tool Co., in 1928. Most of these buildings still exist, but are occupied now by several smaller companies.

Boy's camp at Rhyl in 1929. Attending were fifty-four sons of Chillington Tool Co. employees and twenty-seven from Josiah Parkes of Willenhall. Along with them were thirteen grown-ups and two cooks.

J. Cross & Sons of 55 Willenhall Road, transport contractors and motor engineers. The three in the doorway are, from left to right: Harry, George and Arthur Cross.

J. Cross & Sons' sizeable fleet of vehicles, with their drivers and mechanics, in 1932. Most of the trucks were Leylands.

A crowd of children who all came from Gough Street, just off Horseley Field and the surrounding area, in the 1930s. Most of them attended Walsall Street school. The photograph was taken near the Three Crowns pub, which was better known as 'Mickey Mooney's'.

The railway offices and beyond them the Queen's Building at the start of Horseley Field. The two girls playing the fool both lived in Gas Yard, just off Union Mill Street. Gas Yard was named after the town's first gasworks, which had been built there in 1821.

The funeral of Harry Parks Temple, wending its way through Lower Horseley Field towards St Matthew's church, in the 1920s.

His fellow sailors carried the coffin, and the crowds were there because Harry Temple had died a hero. Two boys were drowning in a pool near Stow Heath Lane and Harry Temple went in to try and save them. Unfortunately all three lost their lives.

St Matthew's church in the haze behind Harry Temple's coffin as it is carried in. Most of the people who lived in the area at the time have strong memories of the occasion.

Some of the children from the area at the time of Harry Temple's funeral. A class picture at Moseley village school. The only names know are a brother and sister: Ray Moore, on the back row, fifth from the right, and his sister, Ivy, on the second row from the front, also fifth from the right. Third from the right on the front row is Stanley Oldfield.

A section of the school photograph for Willenhall Road junior school, taken in April 1937. The picture features the headmaster and some of the teachers. Willenhall Road school was unusual in that it consisted of infant, junior and senior schools, with about 1,000 pupils in all.

A 1930s montage of photographs of Mr George Breakwell, who owned a café at 165 Horseley Fields. As well as being an accomplished musician himself, he also ran a school of music, and was a clock and watch repairer. Born in 1870, in Chelmarsh, Shropshire, he taught himself all his trades, which included hairdressing.

A Ladies Fellowship Meeting from the Willenhall Road area, in the 1930s. The five ladies seated are, from left to right: Janet Crowe, Mrs Florrie Griffiths, Ivy Colbourne, Mrs Kellagher, Mrs Belham.

Harry Cartwright's greengrocer shop at 120 Horseley Field, in the early 1930s. It closed around 1960, when much of the slum housing in Horseley Fields was being pulled down and his customers were moving away to new estates.

The local Home Guard Company, outside Jenks & Cattell Ltd, during 1942.

Eastfield school choir, in 1949. Miss Hopkins, the music teacher is in the centre of the rear rank. They were about to go to the BBC in Birmingham to sing on *Children's Hour*.

A wedding group outside St Matthew's church in Lower Horseley Fields, having somehow scraped together the clothing coupons for the dresses in December 1946. The former Leah Pritchard of Coventry Street is about to climb in the car, with her brand new husband John James Brew, in his demob suit. To the rear are: Jack Freeman and Bob Winter, the best man, and the bridesmaids are Gwen Porter and Ann Doyle, with little Wendy Freeman at the front.

Another wedding group outside the main door of St Matthew's. This time it is the wedding of Harry Law, in his RAF uniform, and Florrie Rogers another resident of Coventry Street. St Matthews was knocked down in the mid 1960s.

A works outing about to set off from the Ever Ready factory, in the 1940s. In the centre is Frank Horne who came with the company from London in 1932, when they moved into the old AJS works. He joined the firm in 1918 and retired from the canal works, which is what the Lower Walsall Street factory was known as, in 1967.

Lower Horseley Field, in the early 1970s, with Ever Ready's canal works on the right, and the Bull's Head garage on the left. The road here now dips under the railway, when compared with the picture on page 95.

The Ever Ready office girls, in late 1945. Joan Horne, on the front row in the centre, had just joined the firm as the office junior. Among the products made at the canal works were radios. AJS had also made radios there before them.

The entrance to Ever Ready's canal works, which had previously been AJS and before that the Briton Car Co. These buildings are now occupied by other companies.

The upper part of Horseley Fields, when it was still a thriving shopping area, in July 1975. It was said you could buy anything you wanted in Horseley Fields, a community with all its own shops, pubs and cinema.

The entrance to St James' Square, which was on the right hand side leaving town, and is in the middle of the ring road now. No one knows where the name comes from as the Square predated the church further down Horseley Field.

Some Coventry Street residents before the war in the garden of No. 54. There was nothing but cows and fields beyond the garden until the outskirts of Willenhall were reached. From left to right are: Lily, her mother Elizabeth Pritchard and sisters Leah and Minnie, and Minnie's sons, Brian and Alan.

The top of Horseley Field with Biddlestone's store on the corner and the Mount Zion church further down.

A group of ladies, all from the Old Heath Road area, on a day's outing. Mrs Moore is the lady in the centre.

The Willenhall Road flooded outside the Bethel chapel, in the 1950s. Each of the trees alongside the road was planted in the name of one of the local men who died in the First World War.

The Salvation Army gathered for a photograph at the corner of Corser Street and Lower Horseley Field, around 1950. The reason for the photograph is unknown.

The Coronation Day parade, passing some of the prefabs on the East Park estate, in 1953.

The start of Horseley Fields, with the old railway offices on the left, then the start of Old Mill Street. Piper's Row is to the right.

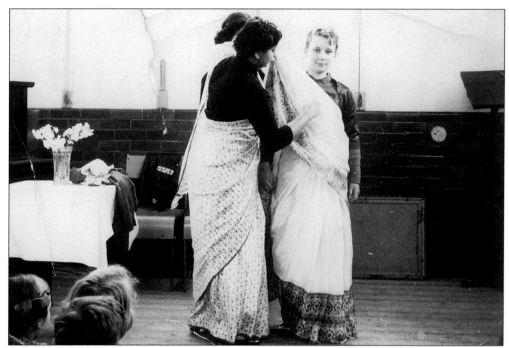

Multi-cultural education at Eastfield school, in 1956. A student from the teacher's training school at Brinsford Lodge is showing pupil Val McGahey how to put on a sari. Val McGahey, after she became Val Willis, taught at Eastfield infants. Eastfield school was the new name for Willenhall Road schools.

The girl's netball team at Eastfield juniors, in the year 1965/6.

The boy's rounders team at Eastfield junior school, in the year 1966. They had apparently just won a cup.

The Sunday school Queen pageant lining up outside the Bethel chapel, with the houses of the East Park estate behind, in the 1960s.

The Union Tap pub being knocked down in June 1964. It was at the junction of Union Mill Street and Horseley Field.

St James' vicarage at the corner of Horseley Field and St James' Street, photographed in 1963. F. Jennings & Son, the funeral directors are next door. The vicarage was built on the other side of St James Street from St James church, in 1843. St James Square, much nearer to town, predates the church.

Charles Henry Brittain Esq standing at the door of his shop at 32 Lower Horseley Field, in the 1960s. It was situated in the block of shops between two pubs, The Stag and The Swan Gardens, and was demolished in the 1980s.

Pupils at Eastfield infants school, wearing tartan ties and dresses, in the 1950s.

The Maypole in Queen Street, in 1955. In these days Danish 'new laid' eggs were 3s 6d for a dozen and home produced were 3s 9d for a dozen. These were also the days when packets of Bird's custard were 10d and the cereal shelf had just Welgar Shredded Wheat and Puffed Wheat and the staff outnumbered customers.

The girls of the Sunday school Queen service at the Bethel chapel pose on the piece of grass opposite the Malt Shovel in the 1960s.

The Little Swan pub, in Horseley Field, in 1973.

The road opposite the Little Swan, in Horseley Field.

A Miles Messenger, G-AHUI, with the ATC, in Wharf Street, in 1971. It was the last aircraft resident at Wolverhampton Airport. It was donated to the ATC but they had to saw the wings off to move it. Amazingly, this aircraft has now been acquired by someone who is rebuilding it to fly once more.

The Teachers of Eastfield infants school, c. 1969. On the back row, from left to right: -?-, Val Willis, Kath Green, -?-, Sarla Chawla, Wendy Raybould, Joan Howell. On the front row: Edith Robinson, Dwina Boldero, Mrs M.E. Laxson (headteacher), Margaret Edwards (deputy head), and Ann ?.

The prefects at Eastfield infants school, in 1971/2. On the back row, from left to right: Mohinder Singh Harbins, Stephen Pugh, Roger Green, Christopher Mitchell. On the front row: Gail Taylor, Susan Bailey, Amba Chawla, Sharon Ruddock.

The Queen's Building, originally built to mark the entrance to Railway Drive and High Level station. It now stands in splendid isolation, the buildings either side having been demolished, and is the entrance to the new bus station.

St Matthew's church being demolished, photographed from the Willenhall Road side, in 1964. As the population of Horseley Fields moved away to the new estates of East Park and Deansfield, the church moved with them and a new St Matthew's was built.

Marlene Burden's last day of work in Ever Ready's drawing office, on 19 October 1966. At the back, from left to right: Gordon Bramall, Ernie Profitt, John Burgess, Sid Wall, Roger Simmonds, John Davies, Brian Davies, Colin Taylor, Clive Lane, and Vic Griffiths. At the front: Rose ?, and Marlene Burden.

Walsall Street school, formerly the Board school, near the junction with Union Street on Walsall Street.

A special service for the 100th Anniversary of the Bethel chapel, in 1990. Mr Jones, the leader of the chapel, is in the pulpit.

Piper's Row and the junction with Queen Street and Horseley Field, in 1973. All the buildings on the left have now been demolished to accommodate the new bus station.

The block of shops, just below The Stag pub in Lower Horseley Field in 1975. They have now been demolished.

These buildings, at the bottom end of Horseley Field, still exist and are some of the few that do. They are occupied now by a multitude of small businesses. Parts of them were built for Edmund Vaughan Stampings, in 1845.

Union Street, looking from Horseley Field, with Walsall Street school in the background, photographed in 1973.

St James' Square looks abandoned and forlorn, as it awaits the bulldozers in 1975. Windows are all boarded up, and the last Triumph Herald is ready to leave. St James' Square was at the heart of the large vibrant community of Horseley Fields, which has now gone completely; no one lives there any more.

Acknowledgements

I have to thank particularly the Willenhall Historical Society for lending me a number of photographs for use in this book and Horace Davies for explaining the significance of some of them. The society meets every month in Willenhall library.

For this book I once more drew heavily on the marvellous postcard collections of Harry Blewitt, a former native of Willenhall, and Mrs B. Walker. I also borrowed a number of pictures from Eric Woolley the well-known Willenhall postcard expert. The wonderful photographs of Reginald Tildesley's company came from Mr David Bate, some of which were used in his book about Tildesley's, *A Fordson Dealer's Portfolio*. A long established company in Horseley Fields, F. Jennings & Sons, lent me many interesting photographs taken over the whole century. Mr D.W. Clare lent me an album of pictures of Horseley Fields taken in the early 1970s, when he went around and photographed almost every building, just in time. Some of the history of the town I derived from Sam and Mary Clayton's wonderful book *Our Town*.

Others to whom I owe thanks, and I sincerely hope I have included everyone are: The redoubtable Mr Jim Boulton, Mrs Leah Brew (née Pritchard), Marlene Burden, Frank Cockfield, Mr D. Crane, Eastfield junior school, Mr John Griffiths, Mr Alex Henshaw, Jack and Doreen Holmes, Mr R.J. Humphries, Mrs C.J. Ison, Harry and Doreen Law, Mrs Marie Laxson, Mrs Doreen Lewis, Mr Arthur Martin, Mrs Vanda Reynaert, Mr and Mrs Trevor Ridgeway, Mrs Joyce Shepherd, Mr Andy Simpson, Mrs June Taylor, Willenhall Town football club, Mrs Val Willis, Mr John Wright, and not least the very patient Wendy Matthiason.